Rookie Read-

The Sun's Family of Planets

By Allan Fowler

Consultants:
Robert L. Hillerich, Ph.D., Bowling Green
State University, Bowling Green, Ohio

Mary Nalbandian, Director of Science,
Chicago Public Schools, Chicago, Illinois

Fay Robinson, Child Development Specialist

ℂ⊃ CHILDRENS PRESS ®

CHICAGO

Design by Beth Herman Design Associates

Library of Congress Cataloging-in-Publication Data

Fowler, Allan
    The sun's family of planets / by Allan Fowler.
      p. cm. –(Rookie read-about science)
    Summary: Provides brief information about each of the nine planets
  that makes up our solar system.
    ISBN 0-516-06004-X
    1. Planets–Juvenile literature. [1. Planets. 2. Solar system.]
  I. Title. II. Series: Fowler, Allan. Rookie read-about science.
QB602.F68 1992
523.4–dc20   92-7405
                                                                 CIP
                                                                  AC

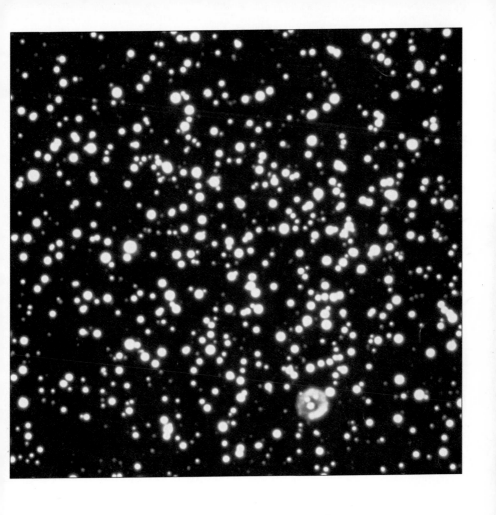

When the night is clear,
you may see many stars.

The stars are very far away.
They look like points of
light.

The Sun is a star, too.
It looks much bigger than
the other stars because we
are so close to it.

5

6

But not every point of light in the sky is a star. Some are planets.

Stars stay in the same part of the sky.

But planets are always
moving — moving around
the Sun.

EARTH

VENUS

MERCURY

SUN SPOTS

MARS

SOLAR PROMINENCE

HE SOLAR SYSTEM

AS SEEN LOOKING TOWARD EARTH FROM THE MOON

The Sun and its family of nine planets are called the Solar System.

Mercury is the planet
closest to the Sun.
You couldn't live there,

or on the second planet,
Venus. They are much
too hot.

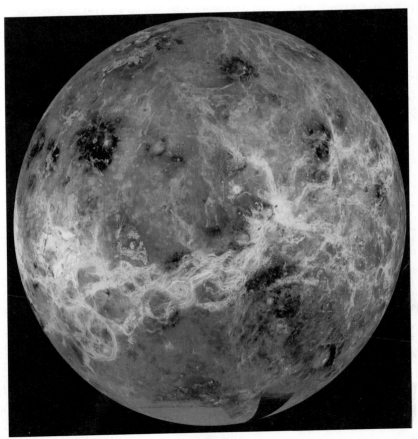

The third planet from the
Sun is neither too hot nor
too cold.

It has plenty of air and
water. So you could live
there...

and, in fact, you do.
The third planet is our
Earth.

Of all the planets in the
Solar System, only Earth is
green with plants and alive
with animals and people.

Mars is the fourth planet
from the Sun. Its air is cold.

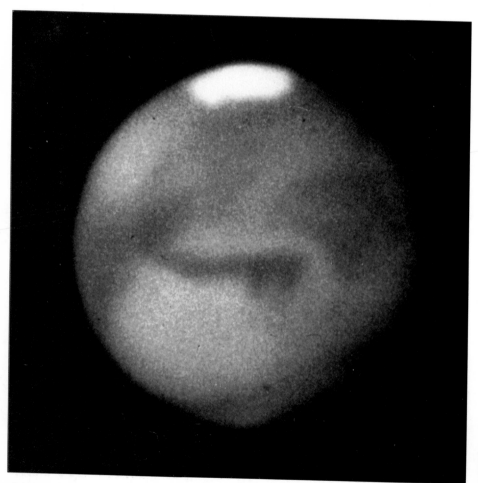

But you might be able to
live there — if you wear
a spacesuit. Mars is covered
with red dust.

Space probes — spaceships
with no people on them —
landed on Mars and took
pictures.

Someday, people from
Earth will travel to Mars
and explore it.

The planets beyond
Mars are much too cold
to live on.

The largest planet is Jupiter.
More than a thousand Earths
could fit inside it.

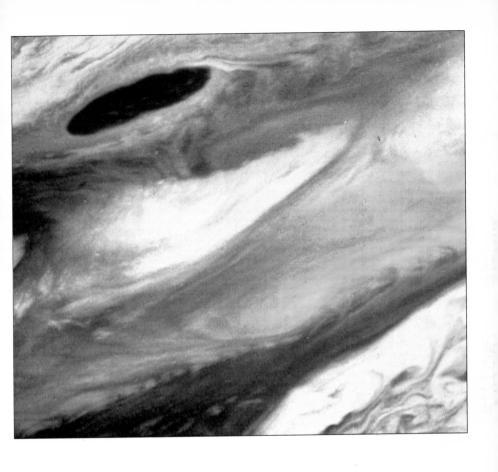

Jupiter is covered by colorful clouds. How many different colors can you see?

The next planet is Saturn.
It has many beautiful rings
around it.

The rings are made of bits
of ice and rock.

Uranus and Neptune have been called twin planets because they are almost the same size.

Uranus gives off a greenish glow. Neptune is bright blue.

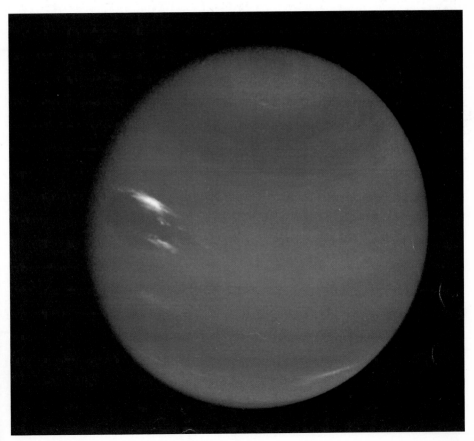

Pluto is the smallest planet and the coldest. Some scientists think it might be solid ice.

Do other stars besides the Sun have planets?

Some people think they do. But no one has found a planet near another star.

Scientists are looking for other planets. But there is still much to learn about the nine planets in our own star's family.

Words You Know

Solar System

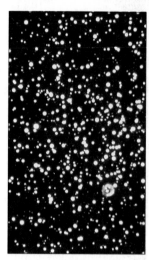

stars

spacesuit

space probe

Sun

30

planets

Mercury

Venus

Earth

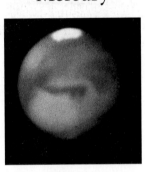

Mars

Jupiter

Saturn

Uranus

Neptune

Pluto

31

Index

About the Author

Allan Fowler is a free-lance writer with a background in advertising. Born in New York, he lives in Chicago now and enjoys traveling.

Photo Credits

NASA – Cover, 3, 6, 17, 26, 29, 30 (top left, top right, bottom left)
NASA-Jet Propulsion Lab – 10, 11, 13, 18, 20, 21, 22, 23, 24, 25, 31 (all photos)
PhotoEdit – ©Myrleen Ferguson, 14
Photri – 5, 30 (bottom right)
COVER: Illustration of the Solar System